MY CAREER IN
THE FASHION INDUSTRY

AN INSIDER'S GUIDE ON HOW TO BECOME A BUYER

fashioncareeradvice.com

CONTENTS

For my husband, N. Daniel Stephen,
who gave me the idea to write this book and whose support has
made it possible for me to live out my dreams.

Many thanks to James David, Deborah Nam-Krane,
Eileen Prince, Ally Ruppel, Philip Ruppel, Jody Saltzman, Byl Thompson,
and Joseph Trimble for your expertise and guidance.
I could not have done this without you.
Special thanks to Renaldo Barnette:
your artwork has made this book come to life.

FORWARD

Much of my early career was trial and error as I figured out what the fashion industry was all about. I am fortunate to have learned from many great leaders who helped me find my way. However, I wish I had known a little bit more about the business going into it.

This is the book I wish I had read when I realized that I wanted to work in fashion. I hope it helps you gain a better understanding of how to get the most out of your career in this exciting industry.

1

MY JOURNEY

I love working in the fashion industry. It's fast-paced, glamorous, and filled with brilliant people. It's a challenging yet rewarding business and keeps me on my toes. I didn't always plan on working in the business, but I am so glad that I ended up here. I feel like I was born to do what I am doing and feel so blessed to have found my professional calling in life.

People always ask me how I got a job in the fashion industry and here is my story.

I thought I was going to be a banker. I went to Northeastern University in Boston, Massachusetts, which has a co-op program. I was required to stay in college for five years and to work full time, in an entry level position in my major, every six months. I majored in Finance and Insurance and worked for a few different finance and insurance companies for my co-op assignments.

At the beginning of my senior year I realized that I didn't want to work in the finance world and was panicked because I had invested so much time getting experience in that field. I wasn't sure what to do but after many long talks with my mother, I decided to pursue a career in fashion. Why fashion? Well, during those long talks with my mother, she would ask me "What do you like to do? What interests you?" I thought about those questions constantly and I knew I loved fashion. I was always up-to-date on all of the current magazines. I loved going to New York to buy my clothes and had strong opinions about what I should wear and what others should, too. So I decided to pursue a career in fashion, not fully understanding what that meant.

After I decided what I wanted to do, I had to start all over again and without as much time as I would have liked. I had to complete one last co-op assignment, and knew that it had to be in the fashion industry.

I thought about what my options were in the Boston area and there were not many. The best option, I thought, would be to work at Louis Boston. Louis was a privately owned boutique that carried the best of the best and was always on the forefront of fashion. It was much like Bergdorf Goodman, but a bit smaller. So I called their Human Resources Manager to see if they would consider hiring me, and they did.

My experience at Louis Boston was amazing. The people who ran it were fabulous. They bought merchandise that they loved and weren't afraid to take a chance on new designers. The product and the aesthetic of the shop floor always came first. While I was there, I spent half of the week on the sales floor as a cashier and the other half in the buying office. I worked for Steven La Guardia, who is one of the most creative merchants out there. At the time he was in his late twenties (which I thought was so old, ha!) and had such a strong point of view about how things should look and what was cool. And he was totally cool.

While I was on the sales floor I would help out with anything needed. I learned how to interact with customers and learned the importance of assisting. My experience at Louis Boston instilled in me a great appreciation of luxury goods and was a phenomenal introduction to the business. From that point on I knew that the fashion industry was the right career path for me.

During that pivotal time I also started talking to some of my professors and asked for advice. One of my favorite professors had a neighbor who lived in Boston and New York half the time because he owned a manufacturing business in the garment district. He told me that if I was serious about a career in fashion, I had to move to New York and get into an executive training program.

After that conversation, I researched all of the major training programs and they all started in May. I wasn't graduating until June. The only one that had rolling admission was Sears. So I applied to the Sears executive training program and got in.

The program was a fantastic learning experience and they relocated me to New York, which was a great perk. However, it was not at all what I expected. The majority of our time was spent working in the store, which was not what I had envisioned. While in the stores, we rotated through different departments like human resources, store operations, visual merchandising, etc. We even spent a week with the receiving department unloading merchandise at six o'clock in the morning. It was very comprehensive training, but the brand was not a good fit for me.

I knew I wanted to move on, so I started looking for new opportunities and answered an ad in the New York Times for a Merchandise Planning Analyst at Barneys New York. I got the job and was thrilled to be working at Barneys! The office was full of hip, young people and *I LOVED* my employee discount. After about six months, I got promoted to Assistant Planner, which made me feel accomplished. Everything was great, but I was a little bored with planning and really wanted to work with product so I needed to do something else.

After I left Barneys I went on to work at Prada as the Assistant Buyer for Men's Ready-to-wear. I was so excited to be there! Everyone in the office was really smart, really pretty, a perfect size two (with a few exceptional size fours), and dressed to kill. It was the most chic environment I had ever been in. It was there that I received my first clothing allowance and it was also the first time I got to travel to Milan for fashion week and attend a runway show. It was a dream come true.

But like everything in life, there is always a flip side. We worked very hard at Prada, often times at the expense of our personal lives. Leaving the office past eight at night was the norm. The trips to Milan were two weeks long and made up of ten to twelve hour days. At Prada, perfection was the standard and anything less was unacceptable. We lived, breathed and were the brand.

While I was there, I had the privilege of working with Connie Darrow, who is a merchandising genius. She was the CEO of the North American region at the time and had been the Creative Director at Prada in Milan prior to that. Connie had incredible vision and knew exactly what an assortment should look like. She set the standard for perfection and would accept nothing less. I was very lucky to have had so much interaction with her.

My experience at Prada was intense and helped define who I am today as a merchant. It also taught me how to do things thoroughly and helped me understand how important it is to work hard.

After Prada, I took a job at Saks Fifth Avenue in the e-commerce division as the merchant for women's accessories. At that time, on-line shopping was nothing like it is today. Back then I don't think most people in America even had an Internet connection at home! It was at Saks that I discovered my love for accessories.

When I left Saks, I started working at Versace, which was something that I had fantasized about since moving to New York. Everything about Versace was over the top and super-duper glam. It was my favorite clothing allowance to date.

A man named Jake Einhorn hired me at Versace. Jake is a retail veteran and brilliant merchant. He trained me to know my facts before opening my mouth and to read selling reports and Women's Wear Daily as soon as I walked into the office each day. Unfortunately, Jake left Versace less than a year after he hired me. However, I learned a great deal from him during our time together.

After Jake left, Versace went through a reorganization. For a while it had a very lean staff, so everyone had to pitch in where needed. It was a hectic time to be there, but it enabled me to become involved in more functions of the business that I wouldn't have been exposed to otherwise.

During my career up until that point I had always been curious about merchandising and product development. I wanted to experience creating products, not just buying and assorting them. This curiosity lead me to my next position, at The Spiegel Brands, a company which has since closed its doors. It wasn't a great fit for me and I stayed there for less than a year. However, I did gain experience developing product and creating a line.

After Spiegel, I had a three-month stint outside of the business and then went on to work at Burberry for five years. I started there as the Women's Shoes,

Handbags, and Accessories Buyer and left as the Director of Merchandising for Men's and Women's Non Apparel and Licensee. Working at Burberry was a coming of age experience. It was as if I walked in as a child and left as an adult. My greatest lesson there was leadership. I had great mentors who helped me discover my personal leadership style.

It's funny; when I was in college I took a class called "Organizational Behavior and Design." I had the most dedicated teacher, Professor McCarty, who was truly involved with her students. She used to say, "leadership is a process, not a property." I didn't really learn what that meant until I took on leadership positions at Burberry.

While I was at Burberry, I was placed into the first high-potential group that they had ever had. We were a group of about forty people from around the world and we would get together a few times a year in London and have a couple of days of leadership training from internal and external senior executives. As part of the program we were able to request mentors. I had the honor of having Stacey Cartwright, the global CFO at the time, as my mentor.

Stacey was the ideal mentor. She made herself available whenever I needed her. She was my partner in my journey as an executive and sincerely cared for my general well-being. Aside from being a wonderful person, Stacey is a shrewd and savvy business leader. I am a firm believer in learning by "osmosis," and just having regular communication with Stacey enhanced my leadership skills and made me a better person.

Another great leader and teacher was my boss. For four-and-a-half of my five years at Burberry, I reported to Daphne Pappas. I learned a great deal from Daphne by working so closely with her for so long. She taught me how to fix a broken business and how to keep healthy businesses successful. She also taught me how to learn from my mistakes and to understand how experiencing failure makes you stronger. Daphne was an inspirational leader and wanted not only to see the business succeed, but also wanted everyone who worked for her to be personally successful.

Also while I was at Burberry, Eugenia Ulasewicz was the
Americas region. She led the organization with great clas
environment where everyone was respected. She knew
and went around the office each morning and made sure
genuinely cared about the people who worked for her. She was a great
strategist and an intelligent leader. Everyone she connected with benefited
tremendously from her leadership.

After Burberry, I briefly worked at Juicy Couture as the Senior Director
of Accessories Merchandising. This was a bit of a change from what I had
done for the majority of my career until then. The customer was younger
and more price sensitive than what I was used to. Also, it was an American
company so all of the decisions were made in our office in New York. It was
a lot of fun developing product and working so closely with design. I got to
work with many talented people and great leaders.

Unfortunately, Juicy Couture was sold and the operations of the company
were dissolved. I was sad to leave such a great team of people, but I am
happy about what happened next. I went on to work at Cache for Jay
Margolis, who exposed me to general management issues that pertained
to more than just merchandising. Jay also taught me about endurance. He
gave one hundred percent to everything he touched and never gave up on
any challenge.

At Cache, I was the Vice President of Accessories Merchandising. It was
almost a continuation of my role at Juicy except at a different brand. I loved
going to work everyday. Developing product and watching it come to life
was exciting and building categories from the ground up was fascinating.

That's my story—so far. The experiences I have had and the people I have
worked with have defined my career. I have learned a lot from what I have
done and am thrilled to keep on learning. As I said earlier, I love my career
and I love the fashion industry. Hopefully, reading this book will help you
find the path that is right for you and help guide you on your journey.

2

PREPARING FOR THE WORKING WORLD

There are a few ways to start your professional relationship with the fashion world. The most common route to getting a job is to go to college and intern at fashion companies. Some people, although not as many, don't go to college and start out by working in a store and transferring into the corporate office. Others start out in a support function and fall into a career in merchandising. However, many companies will only consider applicants with a college degree, which is why the first option is the most common.

Should you choose to go to college, it is one of the most defining times in life. You are working really hard toward something, but the end result is not yet known. The greatest part is that you have time on your side. Take full advantage of it because it will not always be that way. Use as much time as you can to think. Learn about yourself and try to understand what you like and don't like.

Looking back, college was one of the most pivotal times for me professionally. I didn't know it then, but it was when I decided what I wanted to do with my life and started to follow my career path. If I hadn't gotten experience in both the financial and the fashion worlds, it would have taken me longer to figure out what I liked and more importantly, what I didn't like. Ultimately, it would have taken me longer to start working toward my goals.

What to Study in College

You are probably wondering what you should study if you want to become a merchandising executive. In my opinion, it is not necessary to major in fashion merchandising. I studied finance and insurance and my career turned out fine. Buying and merchandising are skills that cannot be taught in a classroom. You have to touch and feel them. Hands-on work experience is the only way to really learn.

Buying/merchandising is a multi-faceted profession that requires many different skills. I recommend studying business administration and selecting a concentration such as finance, marketing, logistics, etc., as all of these areas will become a piece of your job as a merchandising executive. I also strongly suggest that you take a retail math course since retail math is not intuitive and seems foreign to many people outside of the business. During my senior year I took a class that taught the very basic retail math formulas and provided an overview of how an open-to-buy works. (An *open-to-buy* is a tool used to measure inventory productivity and determine inventory needs.) It was extremely helpful when I started working because I already understood the general principles of a major part of my job. If your school does not offer any retail classes, look for a nearby school that does and take a summer or night course.

Whatever you study, make sure to keep your grades up. The fashion industry is very competitive and your grades will matter. I always look at the GPA on resumes. It's a quick way to judge a candidate's ability to achieve and is the only measure available to understand how seriously someone takes his or her work. Always do the best job that you can before and after you start your career.

Work Experience

My college work experiences truly helped define who I am today. Working in finance and insurance made me realize that those environments were not a good fit for me even though I liked the work. And my job at Louis Boston confirmed that the fashion industry was the correct path for me.

Internships and/or part-time jobs are essential no matter what industry you plan to work in. You need to confirm that you really want to work in your chosen industry and the most efficient way to do so is by trying it out before you fully commit. Internships also provide a way for you to get your foot in the door. Employers want to hire people who can start contributing as soon as possible. The more knowledge and skills you have, the faster you can contribute.

You will need references when you are applying for your first job and usually employers want to hear from someone you have interned for.

Internships are also a great way to start your professional network before you start your career. If I have a choice, I prefer to hire people who have worked with or for someone I know.

Retail store experience is also extremely beneficial. If there are not any fashion companies where you live, and if spending your summers in New York is not an option, get a job in retail. Just having names of retailers on your resume will catch the reader's eye. Aside from that, I am always partial to people with retail experience because it is important to understand what it is like to work in a store since that is where it all goes down. Also, people who have worked retail usually have a better understanding of what customers want. If you go this route, try to work at a store that sells merchandise you like. It will make the experience more enjoyable.

Establish Relationships

It is a good idea to gain exposure to as many people in the industry as possible and to start making connections as soon as you can. Talk to people and try to get introduced to fashion industry executives through family friends, etc. If I hadn't ever spoken to my professor's neighbor, I probably would have stayed in Boston after graduation and set my career back a few years.

Other great resources are LinkedIn (I love LinkedIn!) and your school's alumni directory. I have had many requests for advice on how to start a career in fashion through these two vehicles. I even hired someone as an assistant buyer who reached out to me through Northeastern's alumni directory. I have also been hired for a position because a recruiter found me on LinkedIn. Work all the connections you have and never dismiss an introduction.

Required Skills

First and foremost you must be comfortable with math. The underlying purpose of a merchandising executive's professional existence is to make as much money for the company as possible. The more senior your job becomes, the more money is at stake and the more complicated the math gets.

A working knowledge of Excel is also a must. Data and spreadsheets are a major part of any entry level job. If you do not know how to use Excel, learn the basics before you start circulating your resume. Become proficient with pivot tables and VLOOKUP. These functions are an assistant buyer's best friend!

In addition to technical skills, there are also aesthetic requirements. You must have a high taste level that is reflected in the way you present yourself. Look professional at all times. Professional in the fashion world means your hair is neat and you are dressed in stylish clothing, accessories, and shoes. If this is not second nature to you, work really, really hard at it. Go through magazines and pull out pictures of outfits you like and buy clothes and shoes that look like them.

3

INTERVIEWS

Sometimes, the hardest part about interviewing is getting the interview. Once you make it to that stage, take the process very seriously.

The main point of an interview is to impress the potential employer and as the old cliché goes "you never get a second chance to make a first impression." Interviews are a filtering process. As much as employers are trying to find the right person for the job, they are also trying to filter out the ones who are a bad fit. Be sure to put your best foot forward so you can stay in the running and land the job you want.

Look Your Best

What you wear is extremely important. I almost didn't hire a former assistant because I didn't like what she wore to the interview. Make sure that you look as good as, if not better than, the person you are meeting with. Fashion industry executives are hard-wired to make fast, critical decisions based on aesthetics and function (and we notice everything). Choosing staff members is no exception.

Wear the best clothes you have. More importantly, wear the best shoes and handbag you own. You can put together a great looking outfit from almost any brand for not a lot of money, but you can't fake accessories. Borrow from your friends or an online service if you have to.

When I was first starting out, I only had one Prada nylon bag which got old really fast. I remember going on my second interview at Barneys and borrowing my friend's Fendi bag, which took my outfit up a notch. Also, don't wear bad shoes. Even if you have to go cheap, never wear shoes that are in ill-repair. I am not suggesting you break the bank or shop outside of your means, but do the best you can to look the best that you can. You will be much more confident going into the interview.

Conversation

Do your homework. Make sure you are up-to-date on relevant information

PENELOPE'S TIPS

THREE MUST DOS FOR GETTING AN INTERVIEW

1. Make sure your resume looks compelling. It should be visually pleasing, polished and concise. Triple check for spelling and grammar errors and have someone who is used to looking at resumes proofread it.

2. Set up a LinkedIn account and connect with recruiters in the fashion industry.

3. Search your alumni directory (high school and college) for anyone who works in the fashion industry and reach out to him or her.

about the company you are interviewing with. Also, make sure that you know what is going on in the industry in general. Read Women's Wear Daily on the morning of your interview. (Read WWD.com every day as a general rule). Visit at least one of the company's retail locations before your meeting. (I always ask candidates, "Have you been to any of our stores?" The correct answer is "yes".) Be able to share thoughtful comments about your visit. Another question I always ask: "Who is your favorite designer?" and the answer should not be the head designer for the brand you are interviewing with unless you really, really mean it; otherwise, it sounds insincere.

Last, but not least, *BE YOURSELF*. Do not fall into the "I am who I think you want me to be" syndrome. If it isn't a good fit, it is much better for both parties to figure that out at the interview and not waste anyone's time.

Be sure to send a thank-you note or email after your interview. I like to wait until the next day because it gives the interviewer another reason to think about me the day after the meeting. That's just me. Do what feels right for you, but just make sure you acknowledge the meeting with a thank-you whether you want the job or not.

PENELOPE'S TIPS

INTERVIEW ESSENTIALS

1. Do your homework: learn as much as you can about the company you are interviewing with including visiting their stores.

2. Look your best. Dress to impress.

3. Speak professionally and be yourself.

4. Bring extra copies of your resume.

5. Send a thank-you note.

4

STARTING OUT

The fashion industry is not always a kind place. The sooner you learn that, the better off you will be. If you start your career with a tough job, everything after that will seem easier and you will appreciate what you have. This might not make sense to you now, but I guarantee it will later.

Your first real work experience should be similar to boot camp. Do not be afraid of hard work; embrace it and learn from it. If given the choice, join a glamorous, hardworking company. You will benefit from it throughout your career. Working hard while being chic is an invaluable discipline to master.

An executive training program at a department store (which is very similar to boot camp) is also a great starting point. Training programs usually last between six months to one year and are quite comprehensive. Again, this will be hard work. Not only will you learn retail math and how to use computer systems, you will also have to work in the store folding sweaters and work long, hard hours on the floor during the holidays. All of this will build character and make you a better executive.

The First 90 Days

Most companies treat the first ninety days of employment as a probationary period. This means that your employment can be terminated for any reason within that time period. Aside from that, it takes about three months for someone to get to know you and what you're made of. It is a continuation of the first impression and to some extent the interview.

Attitude Toward Work

The first five years in any industry are spent proving yourself and learning. Experience is the most important teacher and is not something that can be rushed. During your first few years it is important to be humble and work hard. Take on as much as you possibly can. Do not complain about your workload or try to be selective about what you are working on. On the flip side, do not tolerate inappropriate behavior (yelling, throwing things,

PENELOPE'S TIPS

DOS AND DON'TS FOR THE FIRST 90 DAYS

1. Come in early and leave late.

2. Do not become "friends" with *ANYONE*. Be friendly and cordial but do not trust a soul.

3. Remain professional at all times. Do not let your guard down and become casual in any way.

4. Do not plan vacations or days off unless they are made known to your employer when you are hired.

5. Do not check personal email or surf the web while at work. If you need to check on something personal, do it from your phone during lunch.

verbal abuse, sexual advances, racist comments, etc.). Go directly to the human resources department if this occurs.

There is one shortcut (that in fact requires more time) which will help you move ahead faster. It is working long, hard hours and completing tasks that are above and beyond your realm of responsibility. I have had three strong assistants in my career who did this. Each of them worked hard every single day. They would come into the office at eight o'clock in the morning (seven on Mondays) and leave at seven or eight at night (nine or ten on Mondays). They would also discretely come in on weekends to get ahead of the next week. There were times that I thought for sure they were going to die from exhaustion. They worked hard, but after a year they were more than ready to be promoted and were everyone's first choice once something opened up.

Compensation

Do not expect to make a lot of money during the first few years of your career; the first few years in any industry are a learning process. The great thing is that you get to collect a paycheck while you are learning. Think of it as a paid master's program with a clothing allowance.

Don't ever ask for more money just because you feel entitled to it or because your friends in other companies are making more than you. It is tactless and off-putting and will make you seem very junior. If you want or need more money, look for another job at a company that pays more. But always remember that you will have to earn every single dollar you get. Companies do not just hand out money. You are expected to make a contribution in exchange for your paycheck.

Perks and Benefits

The most significant benefit of working in the fashion industry is the enhanced accessibility to merchandise. Every company offers an employee discount of some kind and most luxury brands offer a clothing allowance as part of the compensation package. The degree of the employee discount generally increases as positions become more senior. Important to note: if a clothing allowance is granted, you are expected to wear the clothing to work.

Other benefits vary depending on the level of your position. Some benefits are not clearly defined, but are more of a perk from working in the fashion industry. For example, if you are a buyer, vendors will want to give you things. You will be invited to fashion shows, dinners, parties, etc. Some vendors will extend their discount to you and allow you to write personal orders for merchandise. Some will outright give you merchandise. Be sure to familiarize yourself with your company's gifting policy and stay within the boundaries of it.

5

PROFESSIONAL SKILLS & CHARACTER TRAITS

The following are professional skills and personal qualities that will help you succeed. Don't worry if not all of them come naturally. Some of them will develop over time.

Clear Communication Skills

The ability to communicate accurate and meaningful information is a trait that is crucial to one's success. You must be able to clearly and concisely translate facts and figures from reports into recaps that are easy to understand and get the point across. You must also be able to communicate to your customer through the merchandise that you select and develop. For example, if it is all about pink this season you must clearly communicate that to your customers by buying or developing a lot of pink products.

I once had a superstar assistant who could do anything. One time, I asked her to prep information for a critical meeting where I had to provide my boss with the status of a project that I was leading. I gave her the assignment two hours before the meeting thinking that she would come back to me in about an hour with a summary and that there would be enough time for me to ask for any other information that I needed. She came back ten minutes before my meeting and gave me a stack of extremely detailed spreadsheets and reports. The effort was great, but the information was useless since I didn't have time to analyze it. So, I told her to just give me the top-line facts in ninety seconds or less. In those ninety seconds she gave me all the information I needed. And that was all I ever wanted: key facts to base decisions on.

PENELOPE'S TIPS

FOUR TIPS FOR CLEAR AND CONCISE COMMUNICATION

1. Think, talk, and write in bullet points (three or four max) to communicate only key information.

2. Present each key point in thirty seconds or less.

3. Proofread everything you write.

4. Practice all presentations. If you do not have an audience, use a mirror.

Highly Analytical

An important part of your job will be analyzing sales and inventory figures and translating them into a story that is easy to understand. Senior executives do not have time to scrutinize the details of every category of business. They need top-line numbers and a pointed recap so that they can make timely strategic decisions. Your job is to sift through all of the details and provide high-level, meaningful facts that add color to the numbers.

Mathematical Proficiency

Math is a part of any job to some degree. It is definitely an integral part of a merchandising executive's job. The main purpose of your job, no matter what your position is, will be to sell as much merchandise as you can for as high of a profit as possible. In order to do so, you will constantly need to calculate sales, inventory and profit numbers and understand how the numbers all relate to each other.

Strong Presentation and Public Speaking Skills

You must be comfortable speaking in front of a group of people and must also have the ability to clearly articulate your thoughts. You will be expected to present facts and figures at meetings and conduct training seminars at retail stores or in a showroom. People will look to you as the authority with information and you will need to convey your thoughts clearly, concisely, and with confidence. Most importantly, always make sure that everything you present can be substantiated with facts, not just opinions.

Ability to Handle Criticism

People can be unkind and won't always consider your feelings when delivering criticism. And even when criticism is delivered gently and constructively, it never feels great. As a merchandising executive, the success of your business (or lack of) is on display for all to see. Good or bad, your weekly sales numbers will be published for the entire company to view every Monday morning. The merchandise that you have selected or developed is on display to the general public. Any mistakes you make are highly visible. Be prepared to be constantly judged by others and try not to take it personally.

Extreme Flexibility

There are many different parts of a merchandising executive's job. We are constantly pulled in different directions at the same time and everything is always urgent. The fashion industry itself is a living and breathing entity that is constantly evolving. Conditions change rapidly. Therefore, a merchandising executive must always remain flexible and be ready for the next curveball.

Sense of Urgency

Fashion merchandise has a short shelf-life and you must rapidly maximize its productivity before it is useless to you. The clock starts ticking the minute it hits the sales floor. Therefore, everything you do that relates to your merchandise is urgent and must be done immediately. If your boss asks you to run a report, make a phone call, submit an order, etc., it is urgent. People in the fashion industry are used to working in a fast-paced environment and expect things to get done quickly. If you do not treat tasks and projects with a sense of urgency, people around you will become anxious and frustrated and everyone will be uncomfortable.

High Taste Level and Point of View

Merchandising executives need to have great taste and the ability to identify merchandise that people will want to buy. How does one exhibit a high taste level? By selecting attractive clothing and accessories for oneself and putting them together in a compelling way. In other words, you must look the part. Think about it this way: you would never hire a banker or financial advisor with bad credit, so why would anyone ever hire a merchandising executive with bad taste?

Confidence

A key ingredient for success in the fashion industry is confidence. You must completely believe in what you are saying and presenting. The only way to achieve this is by studying your business and getting to the facts before anyone else does. You must also keep abreast of what is going on in the fashion industry outside of where you work. Read WWD.com every morning. Read The New York Times. Go to stores regularly and study what other brands are doing.

I once had someone on my team who presented very well and was confident speaking in front of a group. However, she didn't present accurate facts. She eventually lost all credibility, which also made me look bad as her supervisor. Gain confidence by really knowing your facts and make sure you know what you are talking about; otherwise, you will make yourself look foolish.

Every day that I worked for Jake Einhorn at Versace he would start talking about business and what was going on in the industry the minute I saw him. No matter how early it was, he had already studied selling reports and read WWD from cover to cover. He was always a step ahead of everyone. Because of this, the first thing I started to do every day was study selling reports and read WWD (and tried to avoid him until I had finished). To this day, these are the first things I do when I get to work each morning.

High Level of Organization

When you work in an intense environment, anything can and does happen. There are always surprises. Because of this you must stay organized. With any job, there are the everyday routine tasks that have to be done consistently. Those tasks must be completed quickly and accurately so you can be ready for all of the special surprise projects that get thrown at you. If you do not stay one step ahead, you will quickly find yourself buried.

Personal Conduct

The fashion industry is made up of a small population of people. That population of people gets smaller and smaller as the positions become more senior. I estimate that there are about three degrees of separation amongst everyone in the industry (in New York) on average. When working for a visible brand or retailer, you are a walking representation of the establishment you work for. People who are not involved with the fashion industry are fascinated by it (except in New York) and will want to hear all about your job. Whatever you do will be associated with your employer. You yourself will be very visible due the small size of the population of the industry itself. Therefore, it is important that you protect your private life and behave in a respectable manner. The first thing I do when I receive a prospective employee's resume is Google him or her and look on Facebook or Instagram. I will not interview anyone who has questionable photographs or inappropriate written posts.

Once your reputation is damaged it is difficult to repair. There is a woman I worked with years ago who loved to party. She used to get really drunk when we went out and would stagger home. Everyone I knew at the time had a story about her. To this day, I still think of her as the party girl and don't take her seriously, and so do all of my friends from that time (all of whom still work in the fashion industry). Being the subject of gossip is not fun, so do what you can to avoid it.

Remember: the world is small and unforgiving. There are many people who want your job. Your "friends" who you eat lunch with every day will stab you in the back so they can climb the ladder faster than you. I have seen it happen many times. Don't give anyone any personal information to leverage against you.

Appropriate Behavior at Professional Social Events

There will be many "social" events that you will attend such as vendor dinners and lunches, charity events, office holiday parties, etc. During such events, it is in your best interest to behave professionally. Even though you are not in the office, you are still on the job. Excessive drinking, foul language, and gossiping about coworkers is not acceptable.

Knowledge of What's Going on in the World

The fashion industry is fueled by consumer behavior so it is important to understand what influences consumers' buying decisions. Part of the job of a merchandising executive is to know what people will want next and to make sure it is available at the right time. This would be really easy if we had telepathic powers, but since most of us do not, we need to understand what is going on in the world so we can predict what the next trends will be.

PENELOPE'S TIPS

TOP FIVE SOURCES FOR CURRENT EVENTS AND CULTURE

1. Women's Wear Daily

2. The New York Times

3. E! News

4. Departures Magazine

5. US Weekly

6

SEGMENTS OF THE FASHION INDUSTRY & CAREER PATHS

Segments of the Fashion Industry

There are three main sectors in the fashion world: mass merchandising (Target, Walmart), mid-tier (mall stores: Banana Republic, Macy's) and luxury (Prada, Bergdorf Goodman). Digital/E-commerce has a presence in of all of these sectors. There are pros and cons to all and the path you choose should really come down to personal preference.

The luxury business is the most exclusive and can be difficult to get into because there are fewer jobs and because more people want to work in that area of the business. Starting out in luxury is great for developing a high taste level (although if you don't have one to begin with you aren't getting in the door) and also gives you access to merchandise that you might not be able to afford so early in your career. There is also always travel to Europe at some point and if that appeals to you, it is a great perk.

In both the mid-tier and mass retail sides of the business, it's a little easier to get a job because there are more of these types of companies, especially in the States. There is usually not as much travel involved, which is great if you like to stay local.

The principles of running a business differ greatly between luxury and mid-tier/mass. Luxury is very specific and detail oriented. It is common for buyers to know the names of top clients, what they like, and what sizes they wear. Luxury is built on fewer customers who spend large amounts of money a few times a year. Mid-tier/mass retail is fueled by masses of customers who buy many units of lower priced products. The merchandise is not as specific and needs to appeal to many people; it also has to be priced appropriately. Many decisions are based on statistics and averages.

Internally, luxury companies are design-driven, so as a Buyer you might not have a lot of input into what the products are. However, the merchandise is usually beautiful and a pleasure to work with. Mid-tier/mass retail companies are more merchant-driven and as a Buyer you will play a major role in what products get developed.

I like both sides of the business for very different reasons. Luxury will always be my first love and I adore it because of the product. When done correctly, the merchandise is beautiful and has personality. Each piece is a work of art and adds something special to your life. Luxury goods evoke emotion and make you feel a certain way when you own them. Working with luxury goods makes every day fabulous. Being surrounded by beautiful things and having the ability to help bring that joy to others is an amazing feeling. Luxury goods are special, which is why it is a privilege to own them.

I don't have experience with mass merchandise, but I love mid-tier merchandise because it is so much fun to work with! Since there is a lot of it, it isn't meant to be perfect. There is room to experiment, see what sells best and run after more of what works. The key to success is having more hits than misses and capitalizing on overarching successes. Sounds easy, right? Wrong. It is extremely puzzling to try and figure out what the customer will like (even when you know you are not going to be completely correct), get in the right amount of it at the right time, and run a profitable business. It's like walking on a tight rope. So why would anyone like doing this? For the sport of it. It's like being on an athletic team where every day is game day and whichever brand's cash register rings in the most sales that day wins. Also, bringing to life a product that many people want to buy is a great feeling.

Working with Jay Margolis has made me look at my job as a sport. He taught me that when your "play" isn't working, it is time for a new move. The rules aren't set in stone and sometimes you need a "game-changer" to regain your advantage. Also, the game isn't over until it's over. You can't ease up when you are ahead. You have to protect your lead. As with any sport, you don't win every game, but you need to win more than you lose to come out on top.

As I said before, you have to do what feels right for you. Chances are you will touch all parts of the industry at some point in your career. Remember that your first job will definitely not be your last. If you are not happy with what you are doing, don't waste time. Move on. This is true for any situation in life.

Career Paths

There are many careers to be had within the fashion industry. However, other than design, which requires a very specific skill set, the two main paths are buying/merchandising and wholesale. I should also mention planning since it is the most critical partner of the groups that manage merchandise.

Buyers/Merchandisers are responsible for selecting and managing merchandise during every stage of its life. When working for a brand, they are also responsible for making sure the right products get designed and produced. Sounds like lots of fun, right? It is; but it is also one of the greatest responsibilities (if not THE greatest) in the entire company. This group is also accountable for how much profit the merchandise brings into the company. And since the company's sole source of revenue is from selling merchandise, they are basically responsible for the livelihood of the entire organization.

Buying/merchandising is glamorous, fun, and sexy. But it is also high pressure with very high stakes. Many people want to work in this field, but not everyone has the stomach for it. These types of jobs are good for smart, competitive, neurotic, well-rounded, brave people who have thick skin. Buyers and Merchandisers are under constant pressure to deliver amazing product. What do I mean by amazing product? Product that sells and yields high margins. The job of a Buyer/Merchandiser is always under scrutiny and anyone and everyone (who may or may not completely understand how complex the job is) has an opinion about how well the job is getting done.

Wholesale is the sister to buying/merchandising. Wholesale people sell merchandise to stores (department stores, websites, etc.). They too are responsible for making sure that salable product gets designed and produced. They need to reach sales targets and have to help whomever they sell merchandise to reach their profitability targets through the sale of these products. These types of jobs are good for charismatic people who are comfortable with direct confrontation, are passionate about selling and presenting, and genuinely like talking to people.

The planning organization is responsible for the checks and balances system for the merchandise that is being bought or sold. They establish budgets for buying, and sales targets for wholesale and retail stores. They take all of the information available about inventory, sales, and markdowns and put it together to create an open-to-buy, which measures how profitable and productive merchandise is for the company. Planning jobs are good for people who like numbers, are highly proficient with computer systems, and have some interest in product, but don't necessarily want to work directly with it. I must also note that in my personal opinion, everyone in a buying/merchandising role should get experience in planning at some point in their career if they plan on becoming a senior executive.

Merchandising Functions (simplified)

Merchants are responsible for product. Sometimes they are Buyers, and sometimes they develop product, and sometimes both. Merchandisers, in the purest form, work with Designers to ensure that product is salable. Usually, Designers come up with a concept and determine what the overall spirit of the collection will be. Merchandisers then provide Designers with a framework of how many styles of each classification are needed. For example, six skirts, four dresses, ten blouses, etc. Designers then design into the guidelines provided.

After the collection is finalized, Buyers (who can also be the Merchandisers) buy the line for stores. They have a merchandise receipt plan (a budget for what they are going to buy) for each classification and buy accordingly. In addition to making all of the numbers work, the Buyer must also make sure that the merchandise sits well together on the sales floor. They are also responsible for buying the right amount of each style so that there are minimal amounts of merchandise to mark down and enough units of best sellers to maximize the business.

Planning Functions

Planners plan out the season's sales and purchases. They figure out how much merchandise needs to be bought and sold and when it should arrive. They work closely with merchandising executives and wholesale teams. At some companies Planners do the buying. In this case, they generally don't determine the assortments, but decide how much of everything is bought.

Stores

The Stores are the lifeblood of any fashion merchandising organization. None of the work done in the office means anything if the merchandise doesn't sell at retail, even if you work for a company that strictly has wholesale functions. The only reason merchandise exists is for it to be sold in a store (or on-line).

Retail stores are mini-companies within themselves. The sole purpose of a store is to sell products. This merchandise has to go through many stages before it can be sold, and there are many functions that help make this happen: The Shipping and Receiving person unpacks boxes of merchandise and makes sure the stock is accounted for. The Visual Merchandiser then takes the merchandise and displays it on the shop floor in a compelling and organized way. Security teams watch the merchandise to minimize the amount that gets stolen. Sales teams are responsible for turning merchandise into cash by selling it to customers. Then, of course, there is the store's General Manager who is the leader of the store and makes sure that everything happens the way it should. This person usually has a working knowledge of all of the functions explained above.

	Buying	Merchandising
Entry Level Position (Title)	Merchandise Assistant or Assistant Buyer	Merchandise Assistant or Assistant Merchandiser
Key Job Functions	Enter merchandise orders, provide information to retail stores, run and distribute reports, track purchase orders, write business recaps, assist with product training seminars, provide administrative support to the buyer	Monitor merchandise production and shipping, track samples, prepare line sheets and color cards, update style information (pricing, fabric composition, color options), provide administrative support to the merchandiser
Essential Skills	Highly analytical (with qualitative and quantitative information), mathematical proficiency, extreme flexibility, high taste level and point of view (must be confident), ability to clearly articulate thoughts, strong presentation and public speaking skills, must be able to handle criticism (thick skin), highly organized	Detail oriented, strong written and verbal communication skills, highly organized, ability to accurately recap meetings and execute action items with a high sense of urgency, ability to work on many projects simultaneously with a high degree of accuracy
Interaction with Product	Moderate to High	High

OPTIONS CHART

Planning	Wholesale	Retail
Assistant Planner, Planning Analyst, or Allocator	Sales Assistant	Sales Associate or Cashier
Run and distribute selling reports, update open-to-buy, track merchandise deliveries, allocate merchandise to retail stores, provide administrative support to the planner	Assist with wholesale appointments, enter purchase orders, collect selling information from accounts, organize samples, perform various administrative tasks as needed, provide administrative support to the account executive	Interact with customers, maintain merchandise presentation on sales floor, assist with store operations
Highly analytical, ability to learn retail math, strong mathematic proficiency, strong computer skills (particularly in Excel)	Highly organized, detail-oriented, clear communication skills, ability to accurately recap meetings and execute action items with a high sense of urgency, pleasant and personable demeanor, comfortable interacting with many people	Pleasant and personable demeanor, comfortable interacting with many people, extreme flexibility (particularly with schedule), highly organized, patient, accommodating, hospitable
Low to Moderate	High	High

7

LIFESTYLE CHANGES

When you start working full-time, regardless of the job, your life will change. Be prepared for this. One of the most major changes to get used to is the loss of control over your own time. The fashion industry is not a nine-to-five, Monday-thru-Friday business regardless of the career path that you choose. If you work in a retail store, you will need to work on weekends and evenings. In a buying/merchandising office, you will need to travel during weekends and sometimes holidays. Wholesale teams often have to work over weekends setting up the showroom for market (the time period when buyers place orders for an upcoming season) and need to be available to accommodate their customers' schedules. Fashion merchandising is a demanding career. You need to know that going into it and need to really love the business to want to be a part of it.

When you work for or with European designer companies, you have to adapt to a European schedule, which means that you will no longer be able to observe every American holiday. For example, everyone shows Fall in mid to end November, so there is a good chance that you will spend the days leading up to Thanksgiving in Europe. You might even need to spend your Thanksgiving there. Either way, you will most likely need to work on the day after Thanksgiving and possibly that whole weekend. The same is true for Memorial Day, and if you work on the men's side of the business, the 4th of July also.

It is important to understand what you are comfortable with and know that your priorities will change over time. I once had an assistant who was a high performer. She moved to New York by herself, without a job, determined to work in the fashion industry. She caught on quickly and could handle anything I threw her way. She traveled to Europe with me and could write orders independently. She had all of the technical skills needed to be successful, but after a year she quit. The intensity of the job (and New York in general) was a lot for her and she didn't love the fashion industry enough to sacrifice other parts of her life that were more important. I give her so much credit for completely immersing herself in her career and working very hard at it, yet not getting so caught up in it that she forgot who she was and what made her happy. She was wise to be honest with herself and make a conscious decision to move on. Had she not had a firm understanding of who she was, she would not have been able to do so. I can't stress enough how important it is to know yourself and be okay with your feelings.

Another big change is travel. It is rare that a merchandising executive stays on the ground all the time. In addition to buying trips, there is usually travel to domestic stores. The travel can be demanding and intense, especially since the business doesn't stop just because you are not physically there. And when you are traveling for work, you work longer hours than when you are at the office. I have had jobs where I had to work all day in the office, go straight to the airport after work, fly overnight, land in Europe very early in the morning, get to the hotel as fast as I could, shower, get dressed, and go directly to the showroom and work until eight o'clock in the evening. I have also had trips where I have boarded an airplane at six in the morning, landed in a different state at nine, visited five stores, got back on a flight at seven in the evening, landed in New York at eleven and was in the office at nine the next morning. These experiences might sound crazy, but they are actually pretty common.

Travel can be exciting and is very manageable when you are young, but priorities will change as you get older. If you get married, your spouse might want to be a priority in your life and your work schedule might make that difficult. You might also want to have children at some point and might want to experience milestones in your children's lives first-hand. However, you might not be able to because you have to go on a trip or work until midnight during market. These are just a few of the reasons that it is so important to know yourself and make decisions that you are comfortable with. You have to mentally prepare for the fact that you will go through many changes or else you will be caught completely off guard when they happen; again I can't stress enough how important it is to be aware of this and to know yourself.

No matter what changes you go through, try to remain true to who you are. Do not become affected by the industry and confuse your occupational privileges with your personal life. Your true friends and family won't like you better because you get to travel around the world and wear designer clothes. They might think those things are really cool, but it won't change how much they love you, so you shouldn't let these things inflate your self-opinion either.

You must remain true to your character if you want to be an effective leader. Anyone off the street can be a "yes-man" and follow the crowd. Leaders have an independent point of view and are not afraid to express it. The more comfortable you are in your own skin, the further you will go.

8

ETHICS

It is important to operate with a high level of integrity. The minute you start working you will be trusted with confidential information and will have access to merchandise. It's expected that you will not share this information with people outside of your organization. You will also be trusted not to steal company property. In some companies, it is within policy to borrow merchandise (generally samples) for personal use. However, in many it is not. Whatever the rules are, be sure to follow them.

Your employer will also assume that you will show up every day, on time, unless you are legitimately ill, or have some other urgent situation that prevents you from coming to the office. Abuse of sick days is intolerable and indicates a lack of maturity. You are hired for a job because your employer needs someone to perform a function. If you do not take that seriously, there are many other people who will.

Email

Be careful with email. Any and all correspondence that comes through your work email address is the property of your employer. Your employer also has the right to view your personal emails (via Gmail, AOL, etc.) if written or received on a company computer. Therefore, make sure you are comfortable with your boss seeing anything you read or write on your work computer. If you are not, then save those messages until you get home or read/write them on your phone during lunch.

Professionalism

Treat everyone professionally, especially those who assist you (interns, mail room staff, cleaning people, etc.). Each person in an organization makes an important contribution and should be valued. Professional karma is real. If you want to be respected, you must respect others. Also, as you progress in your career, treat your direct reports well or they will not want to work for you.

When I was at Burberry, each morning, Eugenia, our president, would walk the floor and stop at everyone's desk and say good morning. She would also ask about our lives. She remembered when your parents were in town or when it was your child's first day of kindergarten, and she wanted to hear about those events. She genuinely cared about the people working for her and it was evident. She respected us and we respected her, which made all of us want to do the best job we could.

Gifts from External Business Partners

Most organizations have a policy about acceptable gifts. There is usually a threshold dollar amount and anything with a value above that needs to be approved by your team's department head. Adhere to those guidelines. Accepting an expensive gift is not worth losing your job over. Also, many times people will expect preferential treatment in return for an extraordinary gift and you do not want to feel like you owe anyone anything.

Honesty and Confidentiality

Report accurate numbers and facts. Never deliberately falsify figures to make your business look better. Not only is it the wrong thing to do, but it can be unlawful, especially if you work for a publicly traded company. Do not ever share information with competitors or take documents with you when you leave a job. Information that you acquire when working at a company belongs to that company. Taking it or sharing it without permission is theft.

Do not steal, ever. Stealing can and will ruin your reputation. No one wants to hire a thief. There is too much access to merchandise in this business to have to worry about dishonest employees. Theft is one of those things where there are no second chances. When someone is caught stealing, no matter how little or how much, they are fired immediately.

9

YOUR JOURNEY

Your journey begins now, as soon as you finish reading this book. Start your prep work: pull together a few great interview outfits and start looking for ways to get experience.

Work every connection you have and when you start getting called for interviews remember to do your homework. Know your facts about the company you are speaking with. Feel great about what you are wearing and always follow up with a thank-you card or email.

After you get your foot in the door, work really hard. Do the best, most thorough job that you can every day. Come in early and stay late. Learn as much as you can. Do not become overly comfortable; you are there to work first and foremost. Study your business and contribute however you can.

Discover who you are. Learn about different parts of the fashion industry to help better understand your preferences and where you will be happiest. Do you like luxury or mass? Are you most comfortable working with product or do you prefer spreadsheets?

Remember that your life will change whenever you start anything new. Keep that in mind always and stay true to who you are. Be honest with yourself and make decisions accordingly.

Your career is a journey, and no matter where that journey leads you, you have to start somewhere. And in order to become an expert in anything, you have to keep on doing it.

Do what you love and everything will fall into place. You have an exciting career ahead of you and you are going to love it!